W9-ARK-224

To Jane
Love
From Eileen

Christmas 1996

Other books by Exley:
Daughters ...   Missing You ...
True Love ...   Sisters ...
Mothers ...

Published simultaneously in 1996 by Exley Publications in Great
Britain and Exley Giftbooks in the USA.

12 11 10 9 8 7 6 5 4 3 2 1

Border illustrations by Juliette Clarke
Copyright © Helen Exley 1996

ISBN 1-85015-710-3

Edited and pictures selected by Helen Exley.
Designed by Pinpoint Design.
Picture research by P. A. Goldberg and J. M. Clift, Image Select, London.
Typeset by Delta, Watford.
Printed and bound by Tien Wah Ltd., Singapore.

Exley Publications Ltd, 16 Chalk Hill, Watford, Herts. WD1 4BN.
Exley Giftbooks, 232 Madison Avenue, Suite 1206, NY 10016, USA.

· *FOR A* ·
GOOD FRIEND

QUOTATIONS SELECTED BY *H*ELEN EXLEY

EXLEY
NEW YORK • WATFORD, UK

*Y*ou meet your friend, your face brightens -
you have struck gold.

KASSIA

When I see him I feel the joy deep inside me, like
pilgrim who is lost and finds the right way at last

G. LAENEN

Being with you is like walking on a very
clear morning – definitely the sensation
of belonging there.

E. B. WHITE (1899-1985)

My friend peers in on me with merry
Wise face, and though the sky stays dim,
The very light of day, the very
Sun's self comes in with him.

ALGERNON CHARLES SWINBURNE
(1837-1909)

Friendship cheers like a sunbeam; charms
like a good story; inspires like a brave leader;
binds like a golden chain; guides like a
heavenly vision.

NEWELL D. HILLIS

My fellow, my companion,
held most dear,
My soul, my other self, my inward friend.

MARY SIDNEY HERBERT

What is a friend?
A single soul dwelling in two bodies.

ARISTOTLE (384 B.C.-322 B.C.)

In my friend, I find a second self.

ISABEL NORTON

WHAT IS A FRIEND?

A friend never phones in the middle of the serial.

A friend leaves a pie on the kitchen table, a vase of fresh flowers by the bed – and a note to welcome you home.

A friend is the only person you will let into the house when you are Turning Out Drawers.

A friend is the person you turn to when your
family just won't do.

A friend carries a list of books you are searching for.
And you have hers.

A friend cries with you over your little dead cat.

Friends phone you at eleven at night to let you
listen to their nightingale.

PAM BROWN, b.1928

*H*appy is the house that shelters a friend!
It might well be built, like a festal bower or arch,
to entertain him a single day.

RALPH WALDO EMERSON (1803-1882)

Under our thatch, friend,
Place shall abide for you;
Touch but the latch, friend,
The door shall swing wide for you!

NANCY BYRD TURNER (1880-1954)

"Stay" is a charming word in a friend's vocabulary.

LOUISA MAY ALCOTT (1832-1888)

A friend is a person with whom I may
be sincere. Before him I may think aloud.
I am arrived at last in the presence
of a man so real and equal, that I may
drop even those undermost garments
of dissimulation, courtesy, and second
thought, which men never put off, and
may deal with him with the simplicity
and wholeness with which one
chemical atom meets another.

RALPH WALDO EMERSON (1803-1882)

One's friends are that part of the human race
with which one can be human.

GEORGE SANTAYANA (1863-1952)

What is a friend?
I will tell you.
It is a person
with whom you dare
to be yourself.

FRANK CRANE

Your friend is the man who knows all about you,
and still likes you.

ELBERT HUBBARD

*S*eeing a good friend is like going home, or like tasting Mother's cooking. I feel secure, and need not protect myself. "Here," I say, "it is safe, for I am loved."

ARNOLD R. BEISSER, b.1925

Friendship, a dear balm ...
A smile among dark frowns: a beloved light:
A solitude, a refuge, a delight.

PERCY BYSSHE SHELLEY (1792-1822)

We need someone to believe in us – if we do well, we want our work commended, our faith corroborated. The individual who thinks well of you, who keeps his mind on your good qualities, and does not look for flaws, is your friend. Who is my brother? I'll tell you: he is one who recognizes the good in me.

ELBERT HUBBARD

*F*riends do not live in harmony merely,
as some say, but in melody.

HENRY DAVID THOREAU (1817-1862)

No man is the whole of himself;
his friends are the rest of him.

REV. HARRY EMERSON

To like and dislike the same things,
that is indeed true friendship.

SALLUST (86B.C.-34B.C.)

willm 1988

*W*hat can give us more joy than a friend? Even more, is there something we need more?

DESIDERIUS ERASMUS (1465-1536)

… *friendship, the ease of it, it is not something to be taken lightly – nor for granted. Because, after breathing and eating and sleeping, friendships are essential to our survival.*

ADELAIDE BRY

*Who do I phone when the boiler makes a
peculiar noise, the cat has a wheeze, the roses
have black spot, the children have rashes? Who
do I phone when the eldest gets his exam
results, the youngest has fallen miserably in love
and the machine has eaten my bank card?
Who do I
phone when the special iris has flowered at last,
a totally unexpected cheque has arrived and
I've made a plum cake that needs to be eaten?
You.*

PAM BROWN, b.1928

… True Blue Friends … make you feel good and warm; they are automatically on the same wavelength; they feel genuinely sorry and come to your assistance when you're in trouble; you can speak freely to them, you don't have to be on guard; they really listen; they care about what you're doing … the list could go on and on….

ADELAIDE BRY

The reward of friendship is itself.
The man who hopes for anything else does not
understand what true friendship is.

AILRED (AETHELRED) OF RIEVAULX
(c.1110-1167)

The most I can do for my friend is simply to
be his friend. I have no wealth to bestow on
him. If he knows that I am happy in loving
him, he will want no other reward. Is not
friendship divine in this?

HENRY DAVID THOREAU (1817-1862)

I love you because you have done more
than any creed could have done to
make me good, and more than any fate could
have done to make me happy.

ROY CROFT, FROM "TO MY FRIEND"

The ideal friendship is between good people,
and people who share the same virtues.
Leading a good life for the sake of friends,
is the utmost of friendship itself.

ARISTOTLE (384B.C.-322B.C.)

If I mayn't tell you what I feel, what is the use of a friend?

WILLIAM MAKEPEACE THACKERAY
(1811-1863)

One of the qualities I value most in a friend is discretion. You must be able to know that you can be absolutely frank with the person you are talking to. The privilege of confidence binds people together, as does the mutual vulnerability it implies.

ROBIN COOK

By secrecy I mean you both want the habit of telling each other at the moment everything that happens – where you go – and what you do – that free communication of letters and opinions, just as they arise … which is after all the only groundwork of friendship....

MARY ANN LAMB

If two people who love each other let a single instant wedge itself between them, it grows – it becomes a month, a year, a century; it becomes too late.

JEAN GIRAUDOUX (1882-1944)

Little do people perceive what solitude is, and how far it extendeth. For a crowd is not company, and faces are but a gallery of pictures, and talk but a tinkling cymbal, where there is no love.

FRANCIS BACON (1561-1626)

A TRUE FRIEND

True friendship comes when silence between two people is comfortable.

DAVE TYSON GENTRY

*What I cannot love, I overlook.
Is that real friendship?*

ANAÏS NIN (1903-1977)

A true friend is like the refrain of a beautiful song.

F. PATARCA

Nothing can come between true friends.

EURIPIDES (484B.C.-406 B.C.)

No matter where we are we need those
friends who trudge across from their
neighborhoods to ours.

STEPHEN PETERS

We are not primarily put on the earth to
see through one another, but to see one
another through.

PETER DE VRIES, b.1910

Trouble shared is trouble halved.

DOROTHY SAYERS (1893-1957)

Friends unravel most of your troubles very
simply. They switch it on or plug it in or
give it a little kick.
And won't allow you to apologize.
"Made the same mistake last week....
Talk about feeling a fool."

PAM BROWN, b.1928

Friends put the entire world to rights over
a cup of tea and a bun.

CHARLOTTE GRAY, b.1937

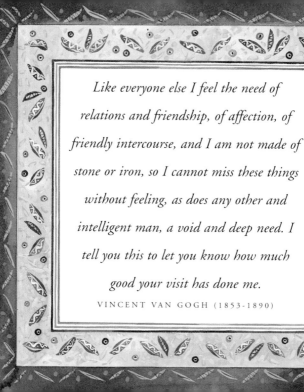

Like everyone else I feel the need of relations and friendship, of affection, of friendly intercourse, and I am not made of stone or iron, so I cannot miss these things without feeling, as does any other and intelligent man, a void and deep need. I tell you this to let you know how much good your visit has done me.

VINCENT VAN GOGH (1853-1890)

Friends don't egg you on to buy things when
you're broke. They say very firmly
"It wouldn't suit you."

PAM BROWN, b.1928

It is one of the blessings of old friends that
you can afford to be stupid with them.

RALPH WALDO EMERSON (1803-1882)

You can always tell a real friend: when you've
made a fool of yourself he doesn't feel you've
done a permanent job.

LAURENCE J. PETER

The mark of perfect Friendship is not
that help will be given when the pinch
comes (of course it will) but that,
having been given, it makes no
difference at all. It was a distraction, an
anomaly. It was a horrible waste of the
time, always too short, that we had
together. Perhaps we had only a couple
of hours in which to talk and, God
bless us, twenty minutes of it has had
to be devoted to affairs.

C. S. LEWIS (1898-1963)

The glory of friendship is not the outstretched hand, nor the kindly smile nor the joy of companionship; it is the spirited inspiration that comes to one when he discovers that someone else believes in him and is willing to trust him with his friendship.

RALPH WALDO EMERSON (1803-1882)

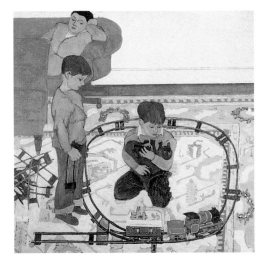

I am like one who went out seeking for
friendship, and found a kingdom.

EDITH WHARTON (1862-1937),
IN A LETTER TO W. MORTON FULLERTON

The moment we indulge our affections, the
earth is metamorphosed: there is no winter, and
no night: all tragedies, all ennuis vanish; all
duties even....

RALPH WALDO EMERSON (1803-1882),
FROM "ESSAYS: FRIENDSHIP"

My friends are my estate.

EMILY DICKINSON (1830-1886)

I trust that even when I'm out of sight I'm not out of mind. Silences and distances are woven into the texture of every true friendship.

ROBERTA ISRAELOFF

Nothing makes the earth seem so spacious as to have friends at a distance; they make the latitudes and the longitudes.

HENRY DAVID THOREAU (1817-1862)

We take our friends with us wherever we go —
and say to ourselves: "They would love this",
"This I must remember to describe", "I wish
that they were here to share this view, this
meal, this small adventure."

PAM BROWN, B.1928

When a person that one loves is in the world
and alive and well … then to miss them
is only a new flavour, a salt sharpness
in experience.

WINIFRED HOLTBY (1895-1935)

One can do without people, but one
has need of a friend.

CHINESE PROVERB

Friendship is a sheltering tree.

SAMUEL TAYLOR COLERIDGE (1772-1834)

When Fortune is fickle, the faithful
friend is found.

QUINTUS ENNIUS (239 B.C.-169 B.C.)

A friend is the one who comes in when
the whole world has gone out.

GRACE PULPIT

So closely interwoven have been our lives, our purposes, and experiences that, separated, we have a feeling of incompleteness – united, such strength of self-assertion that no ordinary obstacles, differences, or dangers ever appear to us insurmountable.

ELIZABETH CADY STANTON

Two people holding each other up like flying buttresses. Two people depending on each other and babying each other and defending each other against the world outside.

ERICA JONG, b.1942

A friendship counting nearly forty years is the finest kind of shade-tree I know.

JAMES RUSSELL LOWELL

May friendship like wine, improve as time advances. And may we always have old wine, old friends, and young cares.

TRADITIONAL

I count myself in nothing else so happy
As in a soul remembering my good friends.

WILLIAM SHAKESPEARE (1564-1616),
FROM "KING RICHARD II"

To meet an old friend in a distant land is like
refreshing rain after a drought.

CHINESE PROVERB

May the hinges of our friendship never rust.

TRADITIONAL

Old books, old wine, old Nankin blue,
All things, in short, to which belong
The charm, the grace that
Time makes strong –
All these I prize, but *(entre nous)*
Old friends are best!

AUSTIN DOBSON (1840-1921)

Lately, in my old age, it has seemed to me, when friends meet to hold a public service to pay tribute to one of their number who has died, that without words to that effect ever being said, they are drawing a circle around that friend. Speaking in turn one after the other, joining themselves together anew, they keep what they know of him intact. As if by words expressed they might turn friendship into magic, the magic that now, so clearly, it had been.

EUDORA WELTY, b.1909

I love tranquil, solitude

And such society

As is quiet, wise and good.

PERCY BYSSHE SHELLEY (1792-1822)

[Friendship is] a general and universal fire,

but temperate and equal, a constant

established heat, all gentle and smooth,

without poignancy or roughness.

MICHEL EYQUEM DE MONTAIGNE
(1533-1592), FROM "OF FRIENDSHIP"

If I don't have friends, then I ain't got nothin'.

BILLIE HOLIDAY (1915-1959)

The man who thinks he can live without others is mistaken; the one who thinks others can't live without him is even more deluded.

HASIDIC SAYING

Life without a friend is like death without a witness.

SPANISH PROVERB

Real friends are our greatest joy and our greatest sorrow. It were almost to be wished that all true and faithful friends should expire on the same day.

FENELON (1651-1715)

What is the opposite of *two*?
A lonely me, a lonely you.

RICHARD WILBUR, b.1921

Without friends, the world is but a wilderness.

ANONYMOUS

*To have even one good friend is to keep
the darkness at bay.*

PAM BROWN, b.1928

*If you have one true friend you have
more than your share.*

THOMAS FULLER (1608-1661)

*No one can develop freely in this world
and find a full life without feeling
understood by at least one person.*

PAUL TOURNIER (1898-1986)

Acknowledgements: The publishers are grateful for permission to reproduce copyright material. While every effort has been made to trace copyright holders, the publishers would be pleased to hear from any not here acknowledged. ADELAIDE BRY: extract from "Friendship, How To Have A Friend And Be A Friend" published by Grosset and Dunlop, 1979. Reprinted by permission of The Putnam Publishing Group; C. S. LEWIS: extract from "The Four Loves: Friendship" published by Fount, a division of HarperCollins Publishers Ltd. © C. S. Lewis Pte. Ltd. 1960; EUDORA WELTY: extract from "Introduction" of "The Norton Book Of Friendship" by Eudora Welty and Ronald A. Sharp © 1991 by Eudora Welty and Ronald A. Sharp. Reprinted with permission of W. W. Norton and Company Inc.

Picture Credits: Exley Publications is very grateful to the following individuals and organizations for permission to reproduce their pictures: Archiv für Kunst (AKG), Bridgeman Art Library (BAL), Chris Beetles (CB), Edimedia (EDM), Fine Art Photographic Library (FAP), Robert Harding (RH), Scala (SCA), Statens Konstmuseer (SK). Cover: Karl Nordstrom, *Siesta i tradgarden,* (SK); title page: Francis Coates Jones, *Reverie on a summer's day,* (FAP) courtesy Anthony Mitchell Paintings, Nottingham; page 8: Luis Graner Arrufi, *The Blue*